LOVE LIFE POETRY

MK AC NEVIN-CROOKS

Copyright © 2016 by MK AC Nevin-Crooks

All rights reserved. No part of this publication may be reproduced, distributed, or transmitted in any form or by any means, including photocopying, recording, or other electronic or mechanical methods, without the prior written permission of the author, except in the case of brief quotations embodied in critical reviews and certain other noncommercial uses permitted by copyright law.

Published by WriterMotive
www.writermotive.com

Written for my Father and Mother -
Tommy & Lily (R.I.P) Nevin.

Thank you for life. For always loving me.
May God bless you both.

In special memory of my loving mother
Celina P Nevin... Lily.

Thank you for teaching me to spread my wings.
For always allowing me to fly. Gone but never
forgotten. Love you forever Mum.
Always in our minds and hearts.

Contents

Contents 5
Forgive 15
Real Life Romance 16
Love 19
Infinite 20
Cuddles 21
Gypsy Heart 22
Still Here 24
Departed 25
Hug 26
Isolation 27
Sorrow 29
Lacking 30
Dance With The Devil 31
Godot 32
Meet Me 33
Mum 34
Death 35
Jump 36
Hard 37
Glorious 38
Let it Pour 39
Drown 41

I Loved You Once 42
Karma 43
Insomnia 45
Hippie Heart 46
Best Friend 47
Instinct 49
Fresh 50
Hate 51
Coffee 52
Dad 53
Icy 55
Happy 56
Leonard Cohen 57
Cherish 58
Girl Gone Missing 60
Hold On 61
Friendship 62
In My Bones 63
Memories 64
Light 65
Hide 66
Pieces 67
In My Head 68
Voiceless 69
My World 71
Joined By Invisible String 72
Free 73

Rise	75
Healed	76
Mouse	77
Kindness	78
Mindfulness	79
Life	80
Dreams	81
Afraid	82
Past	83
Laugh	84
Flickering	85
Love Yourself	86
Peace	87
Change	88
Christmas	89
The Fire Within	90
Be Majestic	91
No Soul	92
Road	93
Compete	94
Dimension	95
Battle	96
Focus	97
Dying	98
Pray	99
Majestic Love	101
Brightness	102

Drowning	103
Be Courageous	104
Barriers	105
Fool	106
Over	107
Raindrops	109
Bad	110
Facade	111
Hell	112
Angst	113
Church Bells	114
Deplore	115
Disappear	116
Flow	117
Devour	118
Rudderless	119
Disappeared	120
Planner	121
Away	122
Negative	123
Deafening	124
All Gone	125
Magic	127
Days	128
Compartment	129
Age	130
Fall	131

Magnificent	132
Regret	133
Dark	134
Fears	135
Dreamer	136
Rejection	137
Bright Side	138
Fickle	139
Dismally	140
What is Death?	141
Buried	142
Save Yourself	143
Courage	144
Rise Again	145
Children	146
Laughter	147
Lead	149
Crazy Gang	150
Cannot Change A Thing	152
Colours	153
Floating	154
Down By The Sea	155
Bruises	156
Being You	157
Awakened	158
The Fire	159
Message From Above	160

Sisters	162
Little Brother	163
Perilous	165
Endless	166
Real Love	167
Narcissism	168
Dig Their Heels In	169
Acidic	170
Teach	171
True Colours	172
Pound Of Flesh	173
Curse	174
Reality	175
Waves Of Pain	176
Fire Within	177
Over The Rainbow	178
Waiting	179
Gossip	180
Winner	181
This Is What We Do	182
Why?	184
Years	185
Weep	187
The Devil	188
Worthwhile	189
The Present	190
Tears	191

User	193
Trees	195
Graves	196
Wander	197
With You	198
Wings	199
Tattered	200
Stand Alone	201
Trapped	202
Despair	203
Grief	204
Sad Eyes	205
Eyes Shine	206
Disappeared	207
Toxic	208
Soulless	209
Grudges	210
The Devil Holds My Hand	211
Torched	213
Stand Up	214
Trust	216
Storm Clouds	217
I Dream	218
Search	219
Wild Sea	220
Suffering	222
Older	223

Who Are You?	224
The Moon	225
Power	226
Solo	227
That Smile	228
What Have You Got?	229
Wedding	231
Vacuous	232
Quietly	233
Swan	234
Time	235
Stubborn	236
Perfection	237
Mask	238
Oceans	239
Pictures	240
Thankful	241
Pointless	243
Oops	244
The Journey	245
Leave You	246
Reject	247
Sweet Dreams	250
Eyes	251
One Last Time	252
Learn	253
Tell Me	254

Tied	255
The Heart	256
You Two	257
Pregnant	258
Staring	259
Love Your Life	260
No More	261
Warrior Queen	262
Glint	263
Over	264
Up and Down	266
Love You	267
Stop	268
Twin Flames	269

Love Life

LOVE

Love is the solution

Laugh

LOVE LIFE

LOVE LIFE

Forgive

Let me dream my spectacular dreams,
Improbable dreams,
You laugh,
You grieve,
You make the choice to truly live.

These thoughts have outlasted everything,
Outgrown the vastness they once resided in,
A wild garden where they have always grown.

My body is old, but my mind is young,
Still a lover of the ridiculous ones.

I shall live on in memories,
Long after my time has gone,
For fun and folly have both been mine,
I grasped them all,
Enjoyed my time.

I dance to the beat of my very own drum,
You may follow me,
This isn't a party for one.

Oh, laughter is the medicine of the day,
To free ourselves from this sadness,
This horrid decay.

A wicked world is where we all do live,
Always make sure you have it within you to forgive.

Real Life Romance

He was a breath of fresh air,
Strong not silent,
He had opinions,
She liked that about him,

He wouldn't take bad behaviour off anybody.
He made her feel protected,
Strong as an ox,
A fighter by trade,
Handsome as can be,
He made her heart speed up just by being.

She had first met him as a young girl,
He was flash,
Had all the cash,
Quick as a hare,
Devilish charm,
Intelligent as can be,
They made a great pair.

When their eyes first locked,
They both knew instantly,
This was true love,
A real life romance,
Together forever or die trying.

He was older of course,
That didn't matter,
It was a real romance,
Lasted over fifty years.

Even in death it did last,
He would have killed for her,
She the same,
They were joined by the heart,
They were never meant to be apart.

When she died,
He did too,
Slowly at first,
His spirit diminished,
Dwindled away,
He could not survive without Lily,
Lily had been strong,
but now she was gone.

He grew lonely without her careful ways,
Her beautiful face,
Her wonderful grace.

He lamented the loss of her soft touch,
Her kindness,
Most of all the elegance she showed whilst being in love,
Only one Lily,
She had been given from above.

It is true what they say…
You don't know what you have until it's gone,
By now she had long gone,
Not by choice,
A horrible accident,
Taken too young.

His heart still lurched,
Every single day a struggle,

He retreats into his head,
Those around him sad as he grows weaker.

He is alone with her inside his head,
He is happy there,
At peace,
Life is good once again,
The numbness has departed,
Love has been restored.

Back together in one another's arms,
His beautiful bride by his side,
As if they were young once more,
Starting out for the first time,
On their long wonderful mystery ride.

Love

We are meant to be loved,
We were not put on this earth to be judged,
It is our birth right to be loved.

We should be able to love others without casting judgement,
Whether someone is worthy or not,
Love is free,
You don't have to use it sparingly.

Infinite

There are miles ahead of us,
Vast lands to investigate,
Together I know we are indestructible,
You are my rock,
My earth,
My moon and stars,
All rolled into one.

When I fall,
When I falter,
I know you will carry me,
Through hills and high waters,
You hold my heart close to yours,
You make everything glitter,
Our love knows no bounds,
Infinite love calls to us,
Ours alone,
Nobody else may touch.

Cuddles

Cuddle them longest,
Cuddle them harder,
Make sure they know,
Just how much they are loved,
That they are the sunshine in your miserable day.

Their little minds so fragile,
Their little faces so cute,
Those expectant eyes look to you for guidance,
Don't let them down,
Be there for them every day.

Be strong for them,
You can do this,
Know that to be true,
Remember, they need you.

Gypsy Heart

I have a gypsy soul,
Nobody can see,
What it's like to be me.

Gypsy heart,
Broken in parts,
Tough as steel,
Is what I appear to be.

Gypsy soul,
I know more,
Than what has gone before.

Free like the wind,
I love to stroll in the sand,
The sea roars,
My third eye is wide open,
I am awake,
Carefree as can be.

Gracious, flirtatious often vivacious,
Nobody gets me,
Or what it is like to be open and yield free.

Softness, kindness, cuteness all enclosed within me,
Gypsy soul is autonomous,
Independent too.

Nobody rules me,
I am free,
Way up high,
Above in the sky,
That's where you can find me.

Don't you want to be just like me?
A gypsy heart,
My soul soars,
It never fears,
Off it goes.

Still Here

I am still here,
I have gone nowhere,
I stroke your hair,
I kiss your head.

I cuddle you in times of need,
I protect you from all those anxieties,
I give you strength,
I shower you in hope,
I push you forwards,
I don't wish you to mope.

You cannot see me,
I know you feel me,
Your hairs stand on end,
I am right beside you,
I never left,
I wish you were not so bereft.

Departed

I know you're still here,
I feel you everywhere,
In the wind in the rain,
I can still smell you in the air.

When my heart feels low,
I know I have my memories which have grown,
I keep you within my tender heart,
Where you were right from the very start.

Sweet Mother though I cannot see you,
You have gone to a kinder place,
I know you are watching over us,
With time we shall be reunited,
I will be back by your side,
In the blink of an eye,
I will no longer cry.

Hug

One more hug,
To heal the bad,
Renew the good.

All the pieces that have broken off,
The ones that chipped away,
You put back together again.

With your touch,
Just by being there,
The pain fades away,
You truly are rare.

Isolation

The howling wind,
The pelting rain,
Ice cold on my skin,
Fearlessly they grow,
Makes me feel the isolation even more.

What a place,
May as well be outer space,
So cold,
The loneliness,
Fills my heart,
Chokes me some more.

Is this how she once felt?
Sitting here staring out at society,
On this leather chair,
No visitors to be seen at all,
Where is everyone?

I was once one of those people,
Running around after life,
Forgetting what mattered to me the most,
Breaks my eternal soul,
All that I let go.

Too busy with life,
Never fitting her in,
Now it's too late,
She has gone.

All that is left is an empty chair,
Where her loveliness once sat and stared,
She is happier now.

Darkness sits there now,
Isolation for the soul resides here,
I can feel it near.

Sorrow

There is a sorrow in you,
So deep-rooted,
It's ingrained into your bones,
I know because I see it in me too.

Sadness drips from your eyes,
You cannot summarise,
All the things that make you feel the demise.

This is how it has always been,
Lived like this since you were seventeen,
You know no other way,
You try to change, but everything just remains the same way.

So now you just accept the bludgeoning that life seems to give to you,
That is just the way you have always been,
So sad to see,
You were meant for greater things,
Instead, you accept all the bad things life brings.

Lacking

You crave to be normal,
To act just like them,
Who wants to be like that?

Admit it to yourself,
You are not meant to mould yourself,
To what their eyes wish to see,
Just be.

You are you,
Unique and true,
Embrace the real you.

Fitting in shows a lack of creativity,
It lacks courage to fit right in,
We should celebrate our differences,
Shows us what we can be,
We can reach for the moon.

Dance With The Devil

The devil likes to dance,
He dances in disguise,
He hides in plain sight,
That is his right.

All the things you ever craved,
He offers them to you on a plate.

You sold your soul,
You just didn't know.

All the things you ever wanted,
Came at too great a price.

Now you are lost,
Still waiting for a reprieve,
It never comes,
You cannot leave.

Godot

All these dreams,
So many aspirations,
Waiting for Godot,
He never appears.

Wasted talents,
Broken heart,
You wish you could go,
Right back at the start.

Meet Me

I am no good at making plans,
They always seem to dissolve somehow,
Or blow up in my hands.

Meet me at the ocean,
Let's do it at dawn,
We shall go for a refreshing swim,
So we can see some more,
Hear the waves roar.

Or a walk in the woods,
We can investigate the autumnal leaves,
You know how those colours make me feel,
I no longer feel misunderstood,
Life doesn't seem so mean.

I'm not one for big romantic gestures,
Though you know I will love you from now,
Until forever.

I speak the truth,
I tell you this,
My heart is yours,
Protect it from now until eternity,
Don't make that an untruth.

Mum

Feeling under the weather,
Nobody here to mind me,
Wish I was back in Ireland,
Knowing my Mum was at home.

Fire roaring below,
She made everything lovely,
So comfortable and warm.

Took all the pain away from me,
Did anything for us,
She always loved us the most,
We were her little angels,
Her cherubs.

Death

You are beneath the trees now,
Staring up towards the diamonds in the sky,
You are always on my mind.

I see the signs,
The butterflies,
The feathers that appear from nowhere,
I know you are there.

I feel you near my face,
Your hands on my head,
I remember all the words you ever said,
I miss your beauty and your grace.

I can no longer see you by my side,
Though my memories keep you alive.

I pray for your soul,
I love you, my dear,
Always near my side.

I miss seeing you with my eyes,
The love I feel for you burns bright,
That love has not died.

Jump

I want to run away,
Start again,
Somewhere new,
A fresh start.

You can move away,
Though that doesn't mean you shall lose those demons,
They follow you around,
Cling to your soul,
They sing the same old boring tunes.

This is your chance,
Escape it all,
Jump whilst you still can,
Before you fall.

Hard

Darkness shines from your eyes,
An instigator of the highest regard,
No smoke without fire,
You are a magician,
You make things appear that are not even here.

I persevere with you,
Even after all the things you do,
I try my best to make amends,
I know we all make mistakes,
You are hard work, though.

You like the rip things down,
Into tiny pieces,
You like to leave a tornado in your wake,
Not happy until it all breaks.

Glorious

Nobody comes close to you,
Not by a mile,
Not a patch on you,
You were glorious,
We all knew.

Nobody looks as good as you,
You were a natural beauty,
Above them all,
Inside and out,
You had it all.

No longer here,
We love you still,
You see our tears,
But what can you do?

We are not children anymore,
You tried your best,
You can do no more,
Your spirit lives on.

Let it Pour

The wind howls,
Oh how it roars,
Like a lion running wild.

My mind is adrift,
The wind whips it aloft,
Expectation and illumination,
Set way up high.

The rain pours down,
Pelts my skin,
I don't care,
It makes me feel wide awake,
I am able to think.

Cobwebs obliterated,
Clarity is felt through my veins,
Horrid thoughts chased away,
Back in the recesses of my brain.

Loved ones,
Long lost,
Alive in my blood,
Every pump,
Every gush,
They are here with me yet,
They are still alive.

When I feel alone,
I pray for the wind,

For the rain,
It is then I regress,
Think of all the things I have done wrong.

I feel so alone,
A prisoner within this mess,
But I hold the key,
To set me free,
One last time,
I open the door,
An escape route I built for myself.

Even when we think we walk alone,
We do not realise,
All the beings that lead us towards the light,
Embracing us tight.

Angels alight,
Beyond the moonlight,
When we cry for help,
They do appear,
Until then I scream for the wind and the rain,
That's where I shall scream my despair.

Drown

I drown again,
In the pain,
Waves of it,
Enveloping my brain.

I fight it,
I try to swim away from my sins,
I weep,
I cry,
I wish it would disappear into the darkest of nights.

Still, it caresses me,
My one,
My only friend,
This really feels like it could be the end.

I Loved You Once

I loved you once,
I couldn't do that again,
You broke my heart,
You twisted the veins,
After that,
I was never the same.

Karma

I broke your heart,
I did not care,
I did not realise karma would be back again,
Angered by my evil spite,
She took delight,
In making me cry until daylight.

LOVE LIFE

Insomnia

Without sleep,
The mind spins into overdrive,
You feel panicked,
What if?
A million worries bubble to the forefront,
No escape.

Insomnia plays with your brain,
You have no idea how to win this game,
The lack of sleep is driving you insane.

Hippie Heart

I have a hippie heart,
It's filled with love and compassion,
Right from the start.

I use it wisely,
I love to move,
Adventure always on the horizon,
I refuse to be abused.

Beauty all around us,
Sunsets and the moon,
I love my beautiful old hippie heart,
It is honest, pure and good.

Best Friend

You know me better than I know myself,
You know all my worries,
All my secrets,
It doesn't put you off,
You still love me like you do,
You still think I'm the best.

You know where the skeletons are,
You helped me hide them,
All the time,
You kept me smiling.

Having you in my life,
I know I am blessed,
God must love me,
He has given me you,
The greatest best friend I could ever wish to meet.

You make me laugh until I cry,
We can be silent together,
Well, maybe for a little while.

Usually, we are busy causing mischief,
Lots of havoc,
I blame you,
You lead me astray,
At least that's what I like to say to you.

Things have always been like this,
We have always been two crazy mavericks,

All the time,
Enjoying each other's madness,
Laughter is near,
When we are together again,
Of that have no fear!

Instinct

I know what I feel,
I shall not be tricked,
Not again.

I follow my instincts,
The signs from my heart,
I listen to those feelings,
I refuse to follow my brain,
Even though those thoughts,
Try to tell me again and again,
What I should do,
How to make good remain.

If something doesn't feel right,
My sixth sense sets in,
I won't fall for your lies ever again.

Fresh

I go to bed,
To try to sleep,
Escape the worries that inflame my brain,
I want to leave them in there.

To fall asleep,
To forget,
To sleep,
To float away from here.

If I sleep,
Maybe I will forget to fall apart,
Maybe I will awaken to a fresh start.

Hate

How can this world be filled with so much pain,
Ruled by hate,
Fuelled by rage,
Makes me sad some people are so inhumane.

Coffee

Waiting,
Always waiting,
For one thing, or another.

For the perfect job,
The perfect love,
The perfect house,
Still waiting,
Anticipating.

Never living life to the full,
Always one break on,
One break off,
Mostly at a standstill.

Today I am waiting for the coffee to kick in,
Then maybe I can be something.

Dad

I love you, Dad,
I shall say that loud and proud,
You are one of a kind.

You have worked so hard,
Always for us,
Your hands show us that,
So do the creases on your face,
From your frowns,
All the lines they make.

Anything you did,
You did it for love,
For our family,
For us.

You taught us how to be strong,
You always helped us along.

If only I could voice these things to you,
Somehow I feel stupid,
So the void follows through.

I love you Dad,
You are the main man,
Nobody comes close,
It's hard to measure up,
To someone who seems to have the most.

I married someone kind,
Reminds me of my lovely mother,
I know you like that,
You know he is sound,
So you bear that in mind,
Every time I am around.

Icy

If only I could tell you,
Just how much I care,
All I see is your icy stare,
So I do not dare.

I try so hard,
It's as though you just want to glare,
Nothing happens,
Words fail,
We just sit and stare.

Happy

Every morning you wake up,
It's your decision to be in a good mood,
Or whether you choose to be in a bad mood.

You have control over your own mind,
Nobody else has that power,
You get to choose whether you win or lose.

A negative mind-set leads you down a perilous path,
A positive mind-set will lead you to the highest mountains.

You can surpass all your dreams,
Just change your mind,
Think happy,
Be happy,
Screw everything else,
This is your life,
Don't mess with it.

Leonard Cohen

We are all broken,
All flawed,
We have irreparable cracks,
We try to cover them up,
Try to hide them,
We pretend they do not exist at all,
It's all a lie, though.

Without any cracks,
The deep ones,
The ones that seem to shatter our souls,
Break our will,
Make us cry,
They are fleeting,
Where would we be?

The wonderful Leonard Cohen knew,
Without any cracks,
How else would the glorious light get in?

We need the cracks to grow,
It enhances our lives,
For without those breaks,
We would have no light at all,
That is where the darkness lives,
We need the cracks for the light to appear,
So we can fix the darkness within.

Cherish

Those scars remind you,
You are stronger than you think,
They are not flaws but life wounds,
Cherish them,
They are part of your history,
Your strength,
They gave you self-respect.

You have done so much with your life,
Everything you have accomplished has been stratospheric,
You have reached the top in so many things,
You are gifted,
More than most,
You set your mind to things and magic appears.

Everything you have ever tried,
You became the best,
You are focused,
That's your way,
That is not an embellishment,
That is a fact.

You have always kept your morals,
You held onto your good humour,
Never looking down on anyone,
You are respectful,
You are modest,
Your kindness has never left your side,
You are a lovely soul.

Your smile has never wavered,
Not for a second,
All the while,
Being one of the last true greats,
One I am proud to have met.

I have loved every minute of being your friend,
Your stories have kept me awake,
At times when I have struggled to feel alive,
In these dark, dismal studios,
You made sure we always strived for more,
Fun is at your core,
A true legend,
You always soar.

You make sure there is laughter and good faith wherever you go,
A true gentleman,
One I am so happy to know.

Girl Gone Missing

She had so many dreams,
Lots of aspirations,
Then one day,
They all slipped away,
Flew away on the sea air.

It was as if someone had knocked her on the head,
She had allowed the decay to set in,
Filled her with dread.

She used to be stoic,
Now she was neither here nor there,
She had lost herself somewhere.

She had never been treasured,
Always second choice,
Nothing to stare at,
In fact, she resembled a little mouse.

She apologised for her voice,
Sometimes her life,
The sparkle she once had,
Had disappeared by choice.

In its place there were vices,
Ones she could not face,
She lived her life in constant sadness and disgrace.

Hold On

Don't give up,
Though today seems darker than usual,
You think the rain clouds are pouring on you,
That's only your perspective,
Know it's untrue.

Hold on to your fire,
Keep that fighting side,
You have better days ahead of you,
Please believe that my dear.

You think nobody cares,
That is furthest from the truth,
You cannot see that though,
The haze has taken control of you.

You are bright, beautiful, clever and fun,
An inspiration to one and all,
Truthful to a fault,
That makes us love you all the more,
You don't realise that, though.

You need nobody but your own heart,
You are stronger than you think you are,
Hold on tight,
Even this high tide shall subside.

Friendship

We grow older,
We move away,
Find ourselves on a new path,
Sometimes we find we are always looking back.

We lost some friends along the way,
They still hold our hearts,
Now they do that from far away,
They still know our quirks,
We love them still.

We move on,
We grow apart,
Find new friends who steal our hearts,
Until one day,
They too shall depart.

In My Bones

Every night before bed,
I think of you,
You are always in my head.

Out of sight but in my heart,
You are part of me,
You are in my bones,
I know I am not alone.

I will never forget your smile,
Your hug,
Your kindness,
Your kiss.

You know I pray for you,
You understand just how much you are missed,
God bless you, my dear,
I shall see you again,
On another realm.

Memories

One day we will all be but a memory,
Do your best,
To be a good one.

Those few seconds when you are about to lose the head,
Take a deep breath,
Count to ten,
Think,
Start again,
Let love be the drug,
No need for tears,
Nor fears.

Let go of the rage,
Change your ways,
Memories last a lifetime,
Spread love not war,
Don't instil fear in little ones,
They learn what they see,
Help them grow healthily.

Light

Darkness comes easy for me,
I push it away,
I invite the light to fill my insides,
Energise me,
Please, I beg of thee.

I don't want to be in this rut,
I'm tired of the same old emotional cuts.

Hide

That smile hides a multitude of sins,
Nobody sees what hides underneath,
They don't understand the pain you feel,
That laugh hides everything.

You continue to be jovial,
You hide yourself some more,
You keep it all to yourself,
You like to hide your broken soul.

Pieces

Falling to pieces,
Too much to do,
Not enough hours in the day,
So what am I supposed to do?

I can only do what I can do,
Trying my best,
Failing dismally,
Just like I always do.

In My Head

In my head,
I will not be defeated,
By the voices in my head,
Echoing in my brain,
It creates catastrophic waves of pain.

Ecstasy comes easy for me,
It's alive within my soul,
Reaching for a higher way of life,
Never feeling alone,
I have my soul.

Arguments adrift in here,
This place that I call home,
My tired little mind,
Has nowhere to run.

Alone with myself,
I dread the thoughts,
They enter easily,
Refuse to be lost.

I try to throw them out,
Without a doubt,
They beg to stay,
I pray they will leave me be.

Voiceless

Voiceless in a sea of faces,
Scared to speak,
Or state my truth,
In fear that I will lose.

Searching in depth,
For what?
Nobody knows,
It's elusive…
It cannot be found.

I'm Floating high,
Nearer the clouds,
Where I prefer to ride.

Hide away that pretty face,
Those sad green eyes,
Your smile it hides,
A thousand sins,
All the places you have been,
Things you have seen.

Keeping clear of peers,
Confidence at an all-time low,
You know you are what you sow.

Trying to glow,
Aimless and low,
Nothing ever changes,
As much as I long for it,

To be just so…
That's what I long for.

Heart filled with pain,
Laughter spills through,
Radiates the face,
That I once knew.

Isolated from life,
Aspiring for more,
Grasping at straws,
Opening facets of a mind that seem closed,
All the while it continues to grow.

My World

I am filled with flaws,
Too emotional by far,
If I am upset I shall tell you so,
If I am happy I want us all to know!

I am not an easy person to be around,
One minute up,
One second down,
Sometimes happy,
Often down.

Though you stick with me,
As though I am sound,
I want you to know,
You have mended my soul,
Made me realise I am loved.

I hope to God we will make it,
Still hold each other's hands,
Look in one another's eyes,
Still love each other,
Know we are enough.

We are two halves,
Together we are whole,
I have loved you the most,
I will do forevermore.

Joined By Invisible String

Our hearts are joined by time and space,
I feel you still though I cannot see you,
Your gentle laugh,
Your wonderful face,
You are no longer here,
I have lost my saving grace.

We are still joined,
Though all I have are signs,
Which fill my heart with gladness,
Whenever I feel you around.

You were always my blessing,
You were never my lesson to be learned,
The love you gave to me can never be overtook,
I love you still, dear Mother, and though I cannot touch you or hear your melodic voice,
I send you out a billion thoughts of love, of joy and hugs.

Free

Autumn is here,
The trees shall teach us,
How beautiful it is to let go.

When the leaves fall from the branches,
Carried along within the gusts of wind,
To new destinations,
Far and wide,
Their kaleidoscope of colours shall be seen,
For all who care to watch and take it all in.

All the time,
The wonderful colours,
Fly amidst the wind,
Call vibrantly to us.

Show us how fantastic it can be,
To set yourself free,
Travel solo,
All alone.

Just you and the wind,
Side by side,
What a lovely ride.

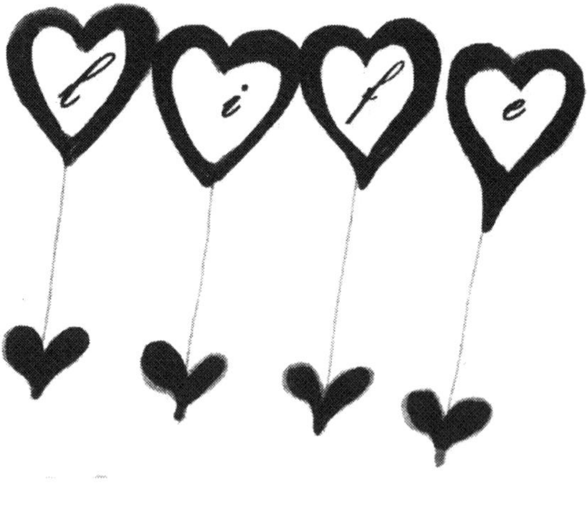
l
i
f
e

Rise

You smile so brightly,
To hide your scars,
You laugh too loudly,
To bring some happiness to those all around.

You don't want anyone to feel how you feel,
So low,
So dark,
So down,
You like to lift people up,
See them rise,
Not rip them down.

You don't want anyone to feel so small,
So tattered,
So torn,
You wish to elevate,
To motivate.

You wish to be the change you never see,
The people who once did this for you,
They have gone,
Now it's just you here alone.

Healed

You loved no matter what,
All the tiny pieces,
You picked them all up,
Stuck them back together.
Healed all the pain,
Made the hurt go away again.

This has always been your way,
Your role is to navigate us through the days,
God bless you,
Thank you for being my friend.

Mouse

It wasn't the first time she had fallen,
She doubted it would be the last,
She rose once again,
From the ashes,
With a spine made from titanium.

A thunderous voice filled her with renewed hope,
She roared now,
The mouse in her had dispersed,
It had disappeared a long time ago.

Kindness

Just be kind,
For no other reason other than because it's a nice way to be.

Don't expect anything in return,
Give wholeheartedly.

Feel the happiness swell,
Your heart shall grow.

All the time knowing,
This is the right seed to sow.

Mindfulness

Curb the desire to disturb people,
Children are young and susceptible,
They learn what you teach,
Cover them in kindness, not your evil bile,
Let them grow up happy without your evil eye.

Life passes by quickly,
Make sure you are a positive influence,
Not a negative vibe,
Life is for living,
Make sure you teach them right.

Words can be harsh,
Watch what you say,
If they were tattooed all over your skin,
Would you still be so quick to say them?

Children are young,
They need your love and care,
Don't hurt them,
Share your love,
Be there.

Life

Doors thud closed,
Keys turn in the lock,
Don't let that demotivate you,
Tick-Tock,
Tick-Tock.

For every fork in the road,
When you think you have,
Been misled,
Only you know the way,
You cannot let it fill you with dread.

It's only when you have,
Suffered loss and tears,
That you know what life,
Really means.

Live each day like it's your last,
Don't let it pass,
In the whizz of an eye,
Its worth so much more,
Than you will ever know.

Dreams

We see each other,
Every night without fail,
In our dreams late at night,
We will both be there.

That's where you'll find me,
Call my name,
You will see my face once again.

Where I have always been,
Deep within your brain,
I will see you there.

Afraid

I have grown tired of this skin I wear,
I have decided to shed it,
Start again.

I no longer wish to feel afraid,
All my life,
I have been frightened to shine,
For fear of being hated or worse,
That I may fall down.

I wave goodbye to that rogue,
The one who has held me down too long,
I say 'Au revoir' to that charlatan,
You have dragged me down enough.

I am moving on from you,
I shall leave you behind,
I no longer have any use for you,
I say 'Bye Bye!'

I no longer wish to be a mouse,
I want to be a lion,
To run at the front of the pack.

I am tired of being scared of my own shadow,
I want to be able to protect my own back,
Be the leader of this pack.

Past

You thought it was the end of everything,
Really it was just a chapter that had finished,
A new one was about to begin,
Something more fabulous than anything you had ever dreamed.

First, you had to let go of all you once thought you had known,
You had felt bereft,
Lost out in a storm,
Frightened and alone,
Scared,
Broken and torn.

Then one day,
It had passed,
At long last,
A new adventure was about to start,
Nowadays you forget to think about your past.

Laugh

You say I can't,
I laugh,
I show you I will.

You can talk down to me all you like,
But I have my free will,
You shall not win.

I've shown you time and time again,
I do not quit,
That I never give in.

Flickering

They are all so happy to fit in,
You don't care less,
You never did.

You act upon a whim,
Never boring,
Rarely dim,
Your light is constantly flickering.

Love Yourself

Love yourself,
Even when you're not feeling your best,
Keep going,
Nurture yourself.

If you don't do it?
Who do you expect to do it?
There's nobody else,
No one else cares.

Believe in yourself,
But first, you must start to love yourself.

Peace

The true meaning of success?
Being able to lay your head on your pillow,
Without a care in the world,
Knowing you have peace within your heart,
Understanding that shall never depart.

Change

You are the author of your own life,
You are the hero,
Nobody else.

Anything or anybody holding you back,
Escape them,
You deserve to see the lights sparkle on you,
You are one of a kind,
Unique to the eye.

This is your life,
Change the things you dislike,
After all, tomorrow is not promised,
You may not have another day,
So start today!

Christmas

So you think they are no longer there,
They are because they still care,
They come down from heaven,
Not to give you a scare,
To watch over you all with a loving air.

At Christmas time when you are feeling down,
Leave an empty chair,
So they can be there.

With you still,
You won't see them but know they are there,
Watching everything.

The Fire Within

Why fear the fire?
The one you hold within,
It shows your will.

You are an eternal flame,
One to be reckoned with,
You start the fires,
The imaginary ones,
The ones you cannot control at all.

Never startled by the flames,
You roar mightily,
It warms your heart,
Nor are you frightened or scared.

You are the heat that everyone feels,
You start the flames,
See them through until the fire has gone out,
Disappeared,
Then you become ashes once more,
Never alone.

Be Majestic

Be the colour in a sea of grey,
Be the wonderful to the bland,
Be the happy to the sad,
Be the everything to somebody else's nothing.

Be you,
Be carefree,
Be majestic,
Be a warrior,
Be whatever you wish yourself to be.

Be who you were born to be,
Not this shadow you have decided to be,
You are not meant to be this tired crumpled human,
You deserve more.

Your colours are too vibrant to hide,
Share your beauty far and wide.

No Soul

The problem is not you,
It was never you,
They are the problem.

Trying their best to destroy you,
Rip your soul out,
Torment you,
Walk all over you.

There is something missing from them,
No soul,
No heart,
They are the problem, not you,
It was never you.

Keep doing all the good things you do,
Karma bites hard,
They will have their day,
You will be watching and waiting,
Until then,
Remain the same way.

Road

Oh, this winding road,
Paved with beautiful stone,
Easy to walk,
No flowers grow, though.

The sunshine refuses to light the way,
This is normality,
For you,
For me,
This seems to be the mentality.

I just want some madness,
To reignite the fire in my tummy,
To let me see life can be funny,
I don't want mediocrity,
I just crave curiosity.

Compete

I am not interested in competing with you,
That's not how my brain works,
I want us all to win,
I want us all to succeed,
To do great things.

I don't want to squash you on the way up,
I much prefer giving people a leg up,
Help them along the way,
That makes me feel fulfilled.

I'm not a jealous sort,
That's not in my nature,
I prefer to support.

Dimension

I will love you in another life,
Another time,
A different dimension,
We did not work out this time,
We both know we shall,
meet again,
In another life,
Until then,
You can dream of me, my friend.

Battle

Just be kind,
If you cannot be kind,
Then shut your mouth.

You have no idea what is going on in someone else's life,
People hide behind their smiles,
Some hide it better than others.

No reason for you to despise them,
They are giving it their all,
Not to fall.

We are all struggling,
Some make it appear easy,
Some let us see it is hard,
Just take it easy,
We are all different battling our way through this minefield called life.

Be fair,
Be gentle,
Try to soothe the soul,
If you can't do that,
Then say no more.

Focus

Just because everything seems to be falling apart,
Doesn't mean you have to fall apart too,
Pull yourself together.

Focus on the good,
Concentrate on the future,
Just because things are going bad,
It doesn't mean you have to go with them.

Dying

The biggest regret of the dying?
Not following their dreams,
They built so many walls,
Ones they refused to climb,
Made their lives small,
Forgot why they were here at all.

Pray

Until I am granted the wisdom,
To know the difference,
I shall keep my mouth firmly closed.

I shall pray some more,
For absolution of my sins,
For the wisdom to understand the difference,
For more patience,
To be more understanding by far.

Most of all I pray to be better tomorrow than I have been today,
I pray tomorrow shall come again,
Until then I shall continue to pray,
For tomorrow is another day.

Majestic Love

You are love,
It runs through your veins,
It joins us all

Makes us magical,
Fills us with hope,
The laughter it brings us is mesmerising,
Happiness everywhere,
Surrounded by sunsets,
They ignite our mighty hearts

Love makes us flourish,
A never ending seed which breaks free,
The sunshine makes us strong,
The rain helps us grow,
It excites us and we go with the flow

Through the bad, the good, the misunderstood,
We stick together bonded by love,
We are hopeful and happy,
Shining with love.

We share it out,
We sprinkle it all about,
Love makes us bond,
We can never abscond.

Brightness

You see the good in me,
When I've forgotten how,
You lift my spirits,
You make me high.

Your colours are so vibrant and bright,
You give me love,
When I don't know how.

You have me in your sights,
You hold on tight,
Never losing hold of me,
We sail in the sky way up high.

No words need to be spoken,
You have my heart,
Though I am a struggle,
Every day and every night,
I can be callous and impolite.

Your colours shine on,
Your radiant sparkle is good and true,
How did I ever find someone as beautiful as you?
Hold me tight,
Never give up the fight,
My bark is louder than my bite.

Drowning

You chipped away at me,
Until all self-confidence was gone,
You abandoned me,
Left me drowning all alone.

Be Courageous

You are not a hindrance,
You do not bother people just by walking this earth,
You have a right to be here,
Just like everybody else.

Be courageous,
Keep going,
Lift your head,

Walk as though you have not one trouble,
See how life will begin to improve,
Just by being happy with you.

Barriers

You can solve any problem,
With the right attitude,
It is not the problem,
It is your attitude to the problem.

Change your attitude,
See how doors begin to slide open,
Once they were bolted shut,
Now the sun beams down on you.

Any problem can be tackled,
With a good attitude nothing is impossible,
The word itself reads: I'm possible.

Stop creating barriers for yourself,
Drop the bad attitude,
Stop with the pretence,
Just be yourself!

Fool

Certain songs hit my heart,
I'm transported back,
To a time when I was young and wild,
When I thought anything was possible,
I thought I ruled the world.

Back when there were promises of: 'Come what may,
I will always be there,
I will love you,
Until my dying day.'
They were your words,
You used to them all.

I believed you back then,
All that you ever said,
I never thought those eyes would lie,
Not to me.

Yet they always did,
Makes me sad to think too long,
I was a naive fool,
A helpless romantic,
Thought we had something,
You proved me wrong,
Knocked my heart out,
I drifted along,
You broke me some more.

Over

Years have passed us by,
The way time has left us,
Is not a pretty sight.

We kept our laughter,
We threw away the tears,
I know you still think of me,
Even after all these years.

We cannot rewind time,
Nor erase the mistakes we made,
We leave them in the past,
As we use up all our days.

Love lived here once,
The fire burned bright,
Then one day you just got up,
You'd had enough,
You just walked out.

It took years to bandage my heart,
The holes caused me anguish,
Even now the splinters hurt me,
Cause me pain.

As I sit in my rocking chair,
I close my eyes,
I see your face crystal clear,
As if you are still here.

I know I wasn't perfect,
We both caused the arguments,
The havoc that ensued,
I still cannot get over,
Never seeing you.

No fond farewells,
No long goodbyes,
You exited my life,
As if you were a butterfly.

Raindrops

Remember when the rain used to refresh you?
Now it all it does it depress you.

Long gone are the days when it replenished you,
Now you just sink some more,
The rain drops whack you as they hit the floor,
Drips on you some more,
Until you cannot feel your soul.

Bad

I am not responsible for your happiness,
You try to throw shade where there is none,
You try to cast blame to many.

I am tired of your antics,
You are cruel and unkind,
That is how I have always remembered you,
Nothing has changed.

You dress it up with laughter,
With fake smiles,
I know what hides underneath,
It makes me want to cry,
Every time I look at you,
Another little bit of me dies.

Facade

They made those dents in you,
Without a second thought,
That is how they reach the top.

It will take an eternity for you to beat those dents out,
You carry them around,
They make you frown,
Drag you down,
You wish you had more self-control.

Your heart is battered and bruised,
Though you hide behind a facade of happiness,
It is hard to endure,
This pretend you,
Everyone believes this side of you to be true,
Who are you to tell them the truth?

Though if they really looked at you,
Into those dark eyes,
Especially when you smile,
They would see you have had your soul broken,
So many times,
You have lost count,
The sadness in you,
Is fuelled by all that is lacking in you.

Hell

Better to have loved and lost,
Than never to have found love at all,
It's all a learning curve.

Whatever doesn't kill you makes you stronger,
Allows you to be wiser,
So next time you won't have to lose who you love.

You understand all the pitfalls,
You will navigate them better.

You know the way to wander,
The routes that bring you to nirvana.

No more crying for you,
You waved them days goodbye a long time ago.

You shall not go back there,
It was bad enough at the time,
You have no desire to revisit hell,
You have found your soul again.

Angst

All this noise in my head,
Leaves me feeling half dead,
Why won't it quieten down?
Just for a sec?

Four little hands grabbing at me,
Expectant eyes looking up,
Searching for answers,
That I don't have.

Meant to be a leader,
But stuck in quicksand,
The more I try,
The worse it gets,
I am smothering here in this mess.

Won't someone help me?
Move on from this place?
Less angst,
Maybe less stress?

Church Bells

You are a brittle little thing,
Jagged within,
Your blackness can sear through anything.

You try your best,
To lift your soul,
It's hard to do when you feel you don't have a home.

Constantly searching for something,
God knows what?
You are hollow inside,
You often feel blind.

People like to fool you,
You're a gullible silly little thing,
Still, you try your best to be loving.

These tears don't stop,
Darkness oozes from your heart,
The church bells ring,
Death is calling.

Deplore

You can have your opinion,
Each to their own,
I do not judge anyone.

It's the hate that I deplore,
You are throwing it around,
As if we are within a storm.

Disappear

Don't wave us goodbye,
Not today,
Eternity is for a long, long time,
Those bad thoughts,
Shall eventually die,
Just believe they will, my dear.

You are too young to live your life like this,
How about you just flick that switch?
Change the sadness,
You have no use for those thoughts anymore,
Allow them to go.

Make sure you are happy, not mad,
Your life is too valuable for you to disappear,
We all love you, my dear.

Flow

You started over,
When you had nothing,
Not one thing at all.

You showed courage,
The only way you know,
You don't take any prisoners,
Off you go.

You are not a defeatist,
You won't show your woe,
Only one way to go,
Onwards and upwards,
Nobody disrupts your flow.

Devour

You devour love,
Not happy until there is none,
This is what you have always done.

Rudderless

Today is the day,
To forget the past,
Anything negative,
Leave it behind.

The junk you cling to,
Is pointless,
Drags you down,
Until all you can see is darkness.

You deserve to see the light,
You need happiness in your life,
Stop letting people dictate your thoughts.

You are in control,
Take back your rudderless ship,
Steer yourself to safer shores,
You can do this,
Believe in yourself.

Disappeared

Not the woman I once was,
Rain hits my head,
All heavy now,
Never used to make me frown.

My posture isn't what it used to be,
No self-control,
That left me many years ago.

Glory Hallelujah,
Where have the years gone to?
I had so much promise,
Where did it all disappear to?
Wish it would come home,
It never did return.

Planner

I'm no longer a dreamer,
I am a planner,
Dreams are in your head,
A plan becomes reality.

I shall still dream,
Just as wildly as I always have,
This time though I will also be a planner,
Mapping my thoughts out,
So that they are no longer an afterthought.

Away

I lost my heart,
It never came back,
Hollowness resides there now,
Unrest,
Unruly behaviour,
That's why I feel the need to rest,
Life constantly feels like one huge test.

By the ocean sunset,
You sailed away from me,
On a boat made of laughter,
You left me here,
Stole my sunshine,
Took my light,
You left me with the rain,
Plus a bucket load of spite.

Full steam ahead,
Sunlight streamed in,
Trying never to think of me again,
Though I know for a fact,
In your dreams I remain,
Trapped there in your head,
Replayed, again and again,
Driving you insane.

Negative

You never succumb to your emotions,
You hide them within,
You push them deeper still,
Never knowing,
One day they will lift their heads,
You won't like the noise they make,
They are tired of hiding,
Always having to submit,
They will no longer do it.

Deafening

Who knew one could feel so alone,
Whilst surrounded by so many souls,
The ones that preach they care.

Where are they then?
Especially when you need a friend?
All that they send is dead air.

Better to be happy in your own company,
Than surrounded by people who pretend they love you,
Worse still say they care.

The quietness is deafening,
Left alone with the cold winter air.

All Gone

You never loved me,
You just said you did,
I drank it all down,
Like some ice cold liquid.

I gave it my all,
I gave it my best,
It wasn't enough,
You were filled with unrest.

The years have gone on,
The years have rolled by,
You think of me often,
Usually with a sigh.

Nothing to be done,
Those days have all gone,
You get mist in your eyes,
When you think of your lies.

LIVE your LIFE

Magic

You crave for magic to appear,
You beg for solutions to the impossible,
Yet you refuse to believe in magic at all.

How can magic ever materialise?
If you constantly fail to believe.

Ask to receive,
Allow your mind to be willing,
Accept that magic is everywhere,
All around us in the air,
You don't need to be surprised,
Just open those eyes.

Days

Days like these,
Everything has gone wrong,
Just give up,
Go back to sleep,
There you can rest your weary head,
A place where you may weep.

Compartment

I'm no longer sad,
No longer shocked by all the things you said,
Nowadays, I realise they were just words,
Silly words,
Words that meant nothing at all.

Anything you said,
They were all lies from your broken soul,
Another broken promise,
To go with all the rest.

I lined them all up on my head,
Thousands of torments,
They all fill me with dread.

I lock the door on that compartment,
You are dead,
Along with all the lies you ever said.

Age

Age has crept up on me,
I still feel how I used to,
In the olden days,
But nowadays the vision in the mirror,
Is not what I used to be,
Where is she?
This younger vision of me.

Where did this person come from?
This old one?
All of a sudden the wrinkles appeared,
Frown and laughter lines are across this face,
They do not disappear anymore,
They remain,
Grow deeper still,
The shadows on this face tells a different tale.

I don't mind,
I am ageing disgracefully,
Having fun aimlessly,
This is my life to live,
I don't care if you judge me,
I am too busy being me,
Feeling free,
Age has given me extra abilities.

Fall

You hide from it all,
Pretend it's not happening,
Then you relive it all.

If only you had been braver,
Realised it's okay to fall,
You would now be over it all,
Instead, you hold on some more,
Refusing to let go at all.

Magnificent

I would follow you,
Wherever it is you wish to roam,
For your promises of folklore,
Encompass my heart,
Those stories make me feel life all the more.

I feel pleased to be alive at all,
To be in your presence,
You are vivacious and lively,
It is a thrill to be around you.

You make my heart race,
As if we are on a mega ride,
One that is heading for outer space.

I would take your hand any time of day or night,
For I know you would never bring me plight,
There is something magnificent in your might,
I hope you never leave my sight.

Regret

You spend so much time regretting,
You forget to live,
You look back to the past so often,
It gnaws you from within.

Never happy,
Always pondering: 'What could have been?',
How about you face your future with such dedication,
Maybe then you would be grateful,
Instead of constantly bitching,
Your head can take no more,
You fill yourself up with dread.

Dark

You take,
Until nothing else remains,
When you give,
It makes you feel hollow within,
Nobody ever taught you the true meaning of generosity,
Your black heart is dark,
Never happy until you pick everyone apart.

Fears

A wish is but a wish,
Just like a kiss is just a kiss,
You are a powerful human being,
You are more than your fears,
Wilder than your dreams.

You can have it all,
If only you believe that to be the case,
This life is not a race,
First we must face our mistakes.

Dreamer

You say I am a dreamer of ridiculous dreams,
You scream they are improbable,
You don't realise that is why I dream!

To flee from this reality,
Is a thing I am able to do happily,
Come fly with me,
Let's abscond together,
Past the huckleberry tree,
Where our dreams will last forever.

Rejection

It's funny how in your dreams,
You still see me,
You hear my laugh,
Though you have not heard that,
In many years,
That's when we parted ways,
You said I made you feel half-crazed,
Though now you seem to miss my face.

Your dreams are vivid,
Wonderful colours,
You awake confused,
What happened?
How can this be?
Didn't she leave me?

Still, the dreams go on and on,
No respite,
You can't let go,
Rejection hurts the soul,
You wanted so much more.

Bright Side

It won't kill you,
To every now and then,
Look on the bright side of life,
Instead of constantly filling yourself with dread.

Your mind is so easily led,
You need to nurture it,
Otherwise, it shall end up dead.

Fickle

Hug tighter,
Love stronger,
Kiss longer.

Tell your loved ones you adore them,
One day they won't be there,
Then you will wonder why you didn't do all these things,
Too late, though,
Time stops for no man.

Wishing you could rewind time,
No chance of that,
Time has ticked on.

Life is a fickle master,
Drags you down,
Remember to enjoy the highs,
The lows fill you with woes,
Ones you never can shake.

They hang off your coat tails,
By then it's too late,
Nothing you can do,
It has become a part of you.

Dismally

To be happy in your own skin,
Now that would be something I'm willing to see,
Never does happen,
Always failing dismally,
Still me,
Falling uncertainly,
Often uncomfortably.

What is Death?

A doorway to another dimension,
Close your eyes,
You are free to fly,
No more plight,
All these superficial problems are out of sight.

Not frightened,
Death may come,
In the blink of an eye,
The soul roams freely,
Gallantly it goes,
Off the beaten track,
To a place nobody knows.

Buried

You died, but when you did,
My sparkle left with you,
When they buried you that day,
I felt as if I had been buried alongside you.

For my heart was no longer in my chest,
It had flown away with you,
Now all that is left is that all encompassing feeling,
The one that makes me feel emotionally bereft.

A hollowness in my body,
A void so deep I cannot even penetrate it,
All these things I feel solemnly,
Every single day.

Then for a glorious split second I forget,
Oh, that is heaven to feel that delay,
To think you are alive,
That I may talk to you once more!

Then I remember,
You have flown away,
All the sadness comes tumbling out,
The pain,
Waves I feel again and again.

Save Yourself

I have tried a thousand times,
To try to tell you,
You can save yourself,
You need nobody else.

You scream,
You shout,
You roar until your heart is about to pour out,
You are drowning,
You need help.

You will not listen,
All you have to do is stand up,
Save yourself,
You need not one soul,
Just yourself,
Stand Up!
For Christ's sake.

Courage

Be courageous,
Just for once,
Find the happiness inside,
Enough of this nonsense.

Be rid of the sadness that dwells in your soul,
You want to laugh,
So make it so.

Rise Again

You are enough,
Remind yourself daily,
Don't let your overactive imagination run wild and drive you crazy.

You are better than you think,
Even though you perceive yourself as small,
Self-pity is a curse,
Brush it off,
Escape it at all costs.

What use is that attitude to anyone?
Get up!
Rise again.
Stronger than before,
You're no use there slumped upon the floor.

Children

I don't care what you think about me,
My children think I'm perfect,
That is all that matters to me.

You can continue with your negativity,
Nothing you say has any power over me,
I'm as happy as can be,
Knowing I have all the love I need,
My family adore me.

Laughter

A pretty face goes a long way,
But I prefer laughter any day.

Looks they fade but personality goes a whole lot further,
A clever mind is a lovely thing but I won't knock you if that's not your thing,

The eyes they hide the wondrous soul,
Many a secret resides there,
Hidden in the darkest recesses,
It's deep down there.

Worries too they come to pass,
After making a home on your face,
A map of how you have lived.

The scars they show you're a warrior,
Nothing has beaten you,
You have come so far!

Your eyes have cried a million tears,
Tiredness consumed you over the years,
You never let it overcome you.

Your positivity radiated through,
Believing in better,
In all that you do,
Remaining true to yourself,
You're nobody's fool,

Starting with self-love,
You overcame everything else.

If source is in your body,
You follow your own rules,
Life is so easy when you throw away the book.

Age grows your courage,
Fearlessness overtakes you,
You go on regardless,
People's opinions don't detain you.

You always mind your own business,
You look after yourself,
Only after that has occurred,
Can you be of any service to anybody else.

Lead

We are worlds apart,
So far removed,
High mountains now stand in our way.

Where once there was love,
All I see now is murky dark mud,
There is no hope here,
Not anymore,
That was lost a long time ago.

You tore all our love apart,
Ripped it up from its roots,
Then you caused a huge storm,
Almost immediately you were gone.

When I think of you now,
I no longer cry,
My chest no longer feels like lead,
It just feels as though you may as well be dead.

Crazy Gang

What you need is…
Some people who will appreciate you,
Ones that love you for being you,
Crazy little you.

You need to be celebrated not ostracised,
Wonderful little you,
That weird smile,
That comical face,
Lovely little you.

You need a gang of misfits,
Ones that you can hang with,
You know the ones,
The kind that are not perfect,
Relaxed and don't want to have outbursts or mad fits.

It won't matter that you talk nonsense,
That you laugh all the hours God gives,
You will be right at home,
No longer alone.

Cannot Change A Thing

Be happy to be yourself,
You are not required to set yourself ablaze,
To keep others warm.

It is not your responsibility to make others happy,
That is their sole purpose,
You can only try your best,
The rest will do what they wish.

You cannot control anything,
Apart from your own happiness,
Make that paramount.

Colours

As you get older,
You don't want to blend in,
You realise it is bland to fit right in.

So what if people don't understand your life?
If they dislike your choices?
That's their problem,
After all, it's your life.

As the years go on,
You care less and less for gossips,
You know you have been blessed.

You are always thankful,
You have been grateful every day of your life,
You're not perfect,
Then you remind yourself,
Perfection is boring.

You have many colours,
You are unique,
That's how you have always lived your days.

You are happy in your own shoes,
Screw anybody who doesn't like you,
That's their insecurities coming through,
That's their problem,
Not yours.

Floating

She saw everyone for what they were,
That didn't deter her,
She remained calm,
Constantly in control.

Her kindness poured through,
She will bring out the best in you,
Some see that as a flaw,
She knows people are sometimes mean because they feel raw.

No judgement,
She will dance with you,
Raise your star,
Make you feel like you are floating on air.

That's her gift,
Don't feel miffed,
She will big you up,
Bring out the best in everyone,
Maybe even the devil,
That's something she revels in.

Down By The Sea

Down by the sea,
That's where you will find me,
Sand in my toes,
That's the feeling I love the most.

The tide steals my bad moods,
It takes them out towards the moon,
The beautiful sea,
Sees me,
It knows my soul,
More than most.

Bruises

All these bruises,
They lead to scars,
Make us realise we lived our lives,
The good and the bad.

We felt every part of it,
Though sometimes it was hard,
We showed up for every day of it,
We cried,
We laughed,
We endured it all.

The scars show us we have lived,
That we have felt every emotion possible,
We never hid.

We wore our bruises as battle scars,
Made us stronger by far,
Made us the stars we are.

Being You

Love me a little more,
Never let me go,
I need your undivided attention,
You don't understand just how much I need that,
though.

Those sweet kisses too,
All the wonderful things you do,
Never stop being you.

Awakened

Keep spreading peace,
Keep sharing your truth,
Do it when they least expect it,
Smother them in love,
They are broken,
They just don't know.

It's not your place,
To drag the unawakened into the light,
It's not their fault,
They have no sight.

The Fire

Oh her fire still burns,
Brightly,
Stronger than it ever did before.

All around her,
Flames absorbed them all,
Not her, though,
Her flame took control,
Whilst everyone watched in awe.

Message From Above

I love to talk about the past,
Memories surround us,
We are at one,
Finally,
At long last.

Letters sent,
Were read religiously,
I finally understand what she meant,
At long last,
Nothing but love,
Her message sent from above.

The more you read,
The more you think,
You're filled with happiness,
Those letters fill my heart with joy,
I'm delirious.

You were her world,
She never relented,
Even now you feel her love,
You feel that invisible touch on your head,
Covers you in love from head to toe.

You're not alone,
She never left you,
The silence fills this space,
You are so happy right now,
You feel the need to destroy it,

Scream and shout,
Let her know you know she's around.

You are happy,
You understand,
You have always been loved,
You just didn't realise,
Just how much,
You were her little cherub.

If you knew what you know now,
You would have tried harder a million times,
Now it's just you,
Lost out at sea,
Crying and begging for someone,
Anyone to help you,
It's too late,
Her ship has sailed,
You're left here alone.

Your heart is ailed,
Crying silently,
Nobody listens,
Nobody cares,
Stand up straight,
It's all come too late.

Sisters

Sisters grown from the same garden,
So alike,
Yet so completely different.

Each perfect in their own way,
Special,
Prized,
Beautiful flowers,
Thrive alone or together.

Their colours shine through,
Amazing in their own way,
No two the same.

Little Brother

Only one little brother,
I never did get another,
Fast and furious,
Curly hair everywhere,
Red shorts on a tricycle,
Still makes me smile.

The way we ran until we felt as though we could fly,
Best friends forever,
Until life got in the way,
Old age,
Responsibilities tarnished it one day.

Yet we still have our memories,
Summer sun beating down,
Always together,
What did they call us?
The 'special' ones...

We thought we had it all,
Little did we know all that life would throw at us,
Still we kept on going,
Never slow.

Dancing in the kitchen,
Tennis at all hours,
Swimming too,
These are things we liked to do.

The gardening in the summer rain,
Pulling weeds we never thought would come again,
Perfectionists,
We needed the cash,
We always did have the best laughs.

Though distance is an issue,
You are always in my heart,
Listen to me now,
In years to come...
Nobody can untie our heart strings,
They were knotted years ago,
Never to be undone,
Remember, I told you so.

Perilous

I never understood why I felt things so deeply,
Why my heart seemed to bleed,
Feelings and emotions swept over me,
Took me somewhere well away from here,
I almost felt I was lost out at sea.

For the pain in my heart,
Filled me again and again,
Only to restart,
I often wished I could just cut it out,
Find myself a new heart.

Now, I finally know the reason for my sad soul,
The mournful song that sings to me day and night,
It is always a perilous one.

I finally understand,
It is the creativeness in me,
Trying its best to finally break free.

Endless

You look for me,
Everywhere you go,
Your search for me is endless,
Never ending,
Non-stop,
It is draining.

You are constantly searching for me,
In every soul you ever meet,
Yet they cannot compete.

Real Love

How will you know if it is real love?
Well, it won't run away from you,
It will be happy to stay,
Alongside your heart,
Never to part.

Narcissism

Your narcissism is out of control,
You take it all,
Still, you demand more.

What more can I give?
You have it all,
My heart was not enough,
Now you need my soul.

Dig Their Heels In

The problem is...
You think you can make them change their ways,
They won't change,
They refuse,
Dig their heels in until they bleed.

They cannot change,
They wouldn't even know how,
So why bother to try?
Let them roam free,
They are not the one for thee.

Acidic

Bitter and twisted,
What made you this way?
Your acidic tongue,
Only causes decay.

Teach

Teach your children,
They can be whatever they wish to be.

Most of all...
Teach them that kindness is king for us all,
Make sure they know that,
Before they walk out your door.

True Colours

Those bad days,
The worst ones,
The days that make you cry out in pain,
Are actually the best of days.

They allow you to see people for what they are today,
Shows you their true colours.

All the ones you thought had your back...
Slap you hardest,
Then they attack.

Pound Of Flesh

The Devil likes to laugh,
As he gets his pound of flesh,
You wonder why you always feel isolated,
That's because the devil is obsessive,
He is relentless.

He won't let you go,
He loves your mournful soul,
That's why he's always knocking at your door.

Curse

You say it's a curse,
That I feel too much,
Little do you know,
Your icy soul frightens me to my very core.

Reality

When you want something,
You make it happen,
If not,
You will make excuses.

Until one day they become so tired,
You become so exhausted by it all,
You decide you're ready to make your dreams
become a reality.

Motivation reappears,
You are ready to rid yourself of all those ridiculous
fears,
At long last wipe away those sorrowful tears.

Waves Of Pain

I drown again,
In the pain,
Waves of it,
Enveloping my brain.

I fight it,
I try to swim away from my sins,
I weep,
I cry,
I wish it would disappear into the darkest of nights.

Still, it caresses me,
My one,
My only friend,
This really feels like it could be the end.

Fire Within

Why fear the fire?
The one you hold within,
It shows your will.

You are an eternal flame,
One to be reckoned with,
You start the fires,
The imaginary ones,
The ones you cannot control at all.

Never startled by the flames,
You roar mightily,
It warms your heart,
Nor are you frightened or scared.

You are the heat that everyone feels,
You start the flames,
See them through until the fire has gone out,
Disappeared,
Then you become ashes once more,
Never alone.

Over The Rainbow

Searching for the edge of reason,
My mind escapes me,
I scream treason.

Rainbows magnified in the sky,
Where am I?
Lost in the crowd,
I fly by.

Happy thoughts everywhere,
Don't you worry,
Don't despair.

Life can be long,
But not always fair,
Just breath the air,
And say that prayer.

Waiting

What are we but a stone's throw from death,
No clue as to when or how,
Onwards we trudge,
Endless searching,
Yearning,
For what?
No idea,
All seems lost.

The wind in the trees,
Takes us away from here,
It's freeing,
To listen,
To watch,
To hear the penny drop.

God knows the plan,
We are just pawns in this game of life,
Never knowing,
Always waiting,
For something else,
It never comes along.

We waited too long,
Now life is all but gone,
So to quench our thirsts,
We continue to search.

Gossip

Stop listening to the gossip,
Close your ears,
Turn the other cheek,
They may think you meek,
Probably weak,
Who cares?
There is nothing you can do about it anyway,
Ignore those creeps.

Winner

Sparks fly,
Electricity in the air,
All these things,
You create,
A magnet for one and all.

Everyone wants a piece of you,
You cannot appease them all,
Try your best,
Knowing you shall fall.

You try your hardest,
You shall not falter,
You have discipline on your side,
Dedication too,
You lost it for a while but its back,

You're back on the right track once and for all,
You keep going,
You see the prize,
The end is in sight.

This Is What We Do

All the things we do to ourselves,
Sacrificing our health to make money,
Eventually we must take a break from work to find our health,
It all comes full circle,
Chasing things that never come true,
This is what we do.

Constantly anxious about what's to come,
Battling feelings of inferiority and fear,
We bash our brains some more,
Until we are laying on the floor,
Desolate and doomed,
This is what we do to ourselves,
Chasing things that never appear.

We cannot live in the present,
We are so depressed we choose to live in the past,
Reminisce some more,
Add to our agonies once more,
Replaying things we cannot change,
This is what we do to ourselves,
Thinking about things that are immutable.

So busy worrying about living,
We forget to live,
This is what we do to ourselves,
Then one day we realise,
Time has run out,
We have no more time,

We die unhappy and confused,
This is what we do to ourselves,
Maybe this is what we were like the whole time?
Only God knows,
Certainly not I.

Why?

Why do I cry so much?
I feel too deeply,
I think too much.

Why do I laugh so much?
I love to be joyful,
I love to be the clown,
To feel free,
If only for a second to escape being me.

I love the sound of fun,
Makes me feel young,
Makes me happy,
Then I forget to feel down.

Why do I care so much?
I pay attention to what's going on in the world,
It hurts to watch,
Rips pieces from my heart,
I try to bring laughter,
To heal those broken hearts.

Years

The years have passed us by,
The way time has left us,
Is not a pretty sight.

We kept our laughter,
We threw away the tears,
I know you still think of me,
Even after all these years.

We cannot rewind time,
Nor erase the mistakes we made,
We leave them in the past,
As we use up all our days.

Love lived here once,
The fire burned bright,
Then one day you just got up,
You'd had enough,
You just walked out.

It took years to bandage my heart,
The holes caused me anguish,
Even now the splinters hurt me,
Cause me pain.

As I sit upon my rocking chair,
I close my eyes,
I see your face crystal clear,
As if you are still here.

I know I wasn't perfect,
We both caused the arguments,
The havoc that ensued,
I still cannot get over,
Never seeing you.

No fond farewells,
No long goodbyes,
You exited my life,
As if you were a butterfly.

Weep

Please leave me alone,
I no longer wish to be the mat you walk upon,
As you cross the floor,
To wipe the dirt from your feet,
Oh how many times do you wish to watch me weep?

The Devil

Whisper negative things to me all you like,
I will not listen to the devil on my shoulder,
I am stronger than ever before.

'The storm is approaching. It will eat you alive' He whispers solemnly,
I smile,
I laugh,
I look him squarely in the eye,
'I am not frightened! For I am the storm.' I shout out,
He looks perplexed,
Afraid,
He has lost this battle,
The same way he did last week.

It's a game we like to play,
Today he did not win,
Tomorrow we will start again.

Worthwhile

I miss you already,
I miss your smile,
You make me feel safe,
As though I am worthwhile.

I don't see you so much,
Not anymore,
Though we used to live together,
It was like we were two halves,
Together we were whole.

Now we are grown,
Families of our own,
Friendship still ignites our hearts,
The love we have never grows old.

I am always here,
Though you cannot see me,
I am just on the other side of the phone,
You never have to feel alone,
I will always be your best friend,
Our hearts are tied,
That shall never end.

The Present

Forget the past,
You have spent too long lamenting,
Too long crying over spilt milk,
It's over now,
Gone!
So come on,
Move along.

There is no point dreaming of a better future,
Unless you put in the legwork,
Nothing will change,
It will remain the same,
The same as it ever was.

How about for once,
Just once,
You concentrate on the present?

It's called the present for a reason,
We are gifted with the here and now,
So focus on today,
Make today the best day it can be,
Then tomorrow start again.

We are all given one life,
Tomorrow may not come at all,
Stop messing around,
Make things occur!

Tears

All the tears I've cried,
Over all of your lies,
Surely by now I should have dry eyes?

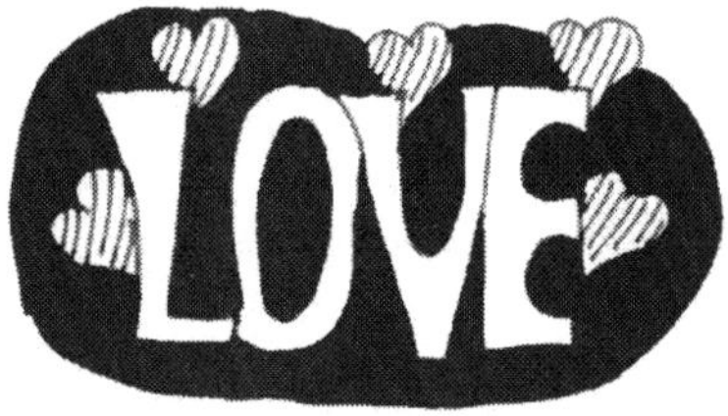
LOVE

User

I'm no longer deemed useful,
You have thrust me from your life,
As though I were a maggot,
You cannot abode to have me within your life.

No time to talk,
No time for anything anymore,
Too busy,
Too important.

It wasn't always that way,
Remember way back when…
We used to laugh and hug,
Talk all day,
Those days have gone,
I'm afraid to say.

You think you are too good for me these days,
Your ivory tower doesn't allow access to the small,
To the insignificant people,
The ones you no longer need to use,
To leap upon,
To climb those steps,
The ones oh so high.

Karma is a funny creature,
One day you are up,
Next day you are down,
I will still be here waiting in line,
For when you fall,

I shall not catch you,
Nor break your fall.

I saw your true colours,
They shone through,
Made me feel utter despair,
You are not worth the time of day,
I do not care for anything you say.

Trees

I am burned out,
Nothing left to rejoice,
Of course, this has been my choice.

This is how I chose to use my voice,
Now all I have is regret and a whole lot of debt,
Money doesn't grow on trees,
I learned this the hard way,
Over all these years.

Graves

Treat people how you wish to be treated,
Manners and civility cost not one thing.

Remember our graves will all be the same size,
Think of this when you are boastful or rude.

Stay humble,
It's good for the soul,
That way your conscience shall never rumble.

Wander

My mind began to wander,
My mind began to roam,
Then one day I realised,
It never did come home.

With You

You cannot see the sunshine,
You choose to close the blinds,
You lock out all the daylight,
You choose to hide.

I shall sit with you,
In the darkness,
All throughout the night.

Then you will always know,
I will be there for you,
That things will be alright.

Wings

She tries her best,
To cut his wings,
She does not realise,
She will never win.

Tattered

I am in love with being in love,
My tattered soul wants to be loved once more,
Searching for another broken heart,
Who can repair me,
Until I depart.

Stand Alone

I would rather be alone,
Than stand with you,
I know you do not value me,
Or anything I do.

So I feel happier being alone,
Than surrounded by people who despise me.

I hate to dumbfound you,
But thought you should know,
I am strong enough to stand alone.

This won't be the first time,
I doubt it shall be the last,
This is what I have always done in the past.

Trapped

Love fills us with hope,
Makes us feel greater than we are,
The joy that runs through our veins,
Remains the same.

It comes and goes,
One day here,
The next it has gone,
Nobody to blame but our own soul.

Some days we work too hard,
Trying to hold it down,
Keep it next to our heart,
However, love won't be told,
It shall not be held prisoner,
It refuses,
It screams,
It roars,
Until love feels torn.

Once love feels trapped,
Off it goes,
Into the skies,
Gleaming as it soars,
Never to be seen again,
Gone forevermore.

Despair

I am in despair,
So much cruelty going on everywhere,
This earth is filled with venom,
Disgusting people wherever I may stare.

Vile human behaviour all causing irreparable damage,
Abusing people who cannot defend themselves,
What has become of the human race?
What have we done to this earth?
This space?

The disregard we show each other makes me want to weep,
No heart anymore,
How can anybody sleep?

A kind soul keeps trying to find the good,
Even within the coldest of hearts,
Though sometimes you have to open your eyes,
To see that maybe there is no goodness inside of some people,
Inside they hold only the blackest of hearts.

Their bleakness is evil,
Their dark is doomed,
No point trying to find the angel inside of a devil,
This is why you will always lose.

Grief

Take it one day at a time,
Don't plan too far ahead,
Take a deep breath,
You're doing as much as you can.

When you think too far ahead,
You scare yourself,
The upset,
The dread,
Fills you to your head.

How can life just carry on?
As if you had never been here at all,
That is the saddest thing,
As if you were not here,
As if you had never existed at all.

Sad Eyes

Sad eyes,
Happy heart,
Ecstatic soul,
You have yourself,
You need nothing else.

Eyes Shine

Those eyes shine so brightly,
Like never before,
Nothing gets in your way anymore.

Your beauty is intrinsic,
People confuse your kindness with weakness,
That is a mistake.

You kill them with kindness,
Then one day you can take no more,
You explode,
You're a wild woman not a saint,
This is the way life goes.

Disappeared

Your eyes are an ocean,
They swallow me whole,
They change colour constantly,
They call out to me,
Right to my core,
They enrich my soul.

Where did you go to my lovely?
Why didn't you follow me?
You said you would follow me to hell and back,
I looked behind me,
You were no longer there anymore,
You had disappeared somewhere along the track.

Toxic

I won't play your game,
Take your toxic energy away,
You cannot harm me,
Not again.

I'm tired of your drama,
You set yourself on fire,
Am I the only one capable of putting out your flames?
So tired of these stupid games.

Soulless

You are soulless,
Leave me alone,
If not,
Leave your stupidity at the door.

Grudges

Grudges serve no purpose at all,
All they do is drag you down some more,
I'm bored of grudges.

I don't want to waste any more of my time,
So instead of a grudge,
You shall become irrelevant in my world.

That's what you now are,
Irrelevant,
Now, get out of my world,
I'm tired of you,
Fed up of all the stupid things you do.

The Devil Holds My Hand

I wish I could leave here and not return,
Rewind the time,
Stop the clock,
I am fearful of the fact I do not feel anything,
Ice entombs my brain,
Frozen to the core,
I freeze out here alone.

Hopelessness fills me,
Horror too,
I feel so isolated and alone,
Is this normal when my house is always noisy and always on the go?

Even the sound of beautiful children laughing cannot calm me,
I am hollow,
Sadness fills me to the bone,
Silence surrounds me.

A great wall I built,
All those years ago,
Stands staunch beside me,
Keeps me alone,
I am home once more.

It's funny when you think you've healed,
The pain seems to have dispersed,
Then it returns but it's harsher than before,
It's never happy until you've crashed upon the floor.

Will there ever be a time when I am,
happy within my own skin?
Not wishing for distractions,
Or the bitter end?

The Devil holds my hand,
He taunts me still.

He won't let go,
He never will.

Torched

Not all those who smile at you are your friends,
They want to know your deepest fears,
They use them against you,
Time and time again.

You are a silly little thing,
As if you like the torture,
You seem to thrive on this action,
You have not learned a thing,
You stupid little thing.

Nobody here to protect you,
Naive little bird,
Just waiting to be burned.

This has always been the way,
You get torched time and time again,
It's sad to see it happen to you every time,
No place left to fly.

No sense at all,
Nobody to love you anymore,
Yet again,
You find yourself alone,
Go cry some more.

Stand Up

Oh, I have loved,
I have lived too,
Sadly not as a gentle thing.

I am not one to let go easily,
I have never been good at that,
I hold on long past the sell by date.

It's as though I am a stray dog,
Not happy until I have been kicked and punished,
As if I think I deserve no better,
No self-worth.

I try to hold onto bonds that were never really bonds,
Really, they were poison to me,
Still, I trusted too deeply,
I drank it all down,
I believed in you,
In all your lies.

I am a gullible fool,
Time and time again,
I fall for the deceit,
Begging to see the good in this hollow world.

There is some good to be found,
Though it is hard to find,
Too many jokers out there with the upper hand.

You show me what you think of me,
The quietness,
The lack of respect,
Then when you need me you think I should just be there,
I have grown tired of your using ways,
Surely you must be ashamed of yourself?

Now it is my time to stand up,
To rebel,
I do not need your selfishness,
Finally, I realise, I deserve more,
Much more than anything you try to dress up as a fancy day out.

A few moments of your time?
Would my anger then subside?
Doubtful,
You did this to us,
You alone.

I no longer see you,
You are a shadow to me now,
A bringer of darkness,
Crass as can be,
Manipulative little you,
Always that lovely smile,
It seems to be glued on.

What you don't understand?
I can read your whole face,
The lies ignite your eyes,
I see it,
It leaves a trace.

Trust

You hurt me more than most,
I gave you my trust,
You thrust it away,
Into the deepest oceans,
So it would decay,
That's where it remains to this day.

Storm Clouds

Not much left to give,
On days like these,
Your soul cries out,
Exhaustion all around,
You know you have tried,
That never seems to be enough,
Not anymore.

Storm clouds overhead,
Gale force winds at your heels,
Thunder and lightning are both near,
Take heed,
Warning hazard lights appear,
Steer clear.

I Dream

My dream is to be near the sea once again,
To walk the sandy shores,
Feel the sun on my skin,
Let the fresh sea breeze do its thing.

To feel the waves surrounding my feet,
As I lose myself in thought,
Thinking of memories long stored before,
Years ago,
When there was no woe.

Just happiness all around,
Ice creams and cuddles,
Fun and sea,
All the things you did with me.

To hear the waves crashing on the shore,
Melts my heart a little more,
The way it did before,
To live in a house overlooking the sea,
That's where I wish I could be,
Just you and me.

Search

I remember the days when love screamed from your soul,
You don't hear that noise much,
Not anymore.

Back in the day when love oozed from your eyes,
I understood it well then.

Nowadays it's rare to see love,
I search for it,
Within your face,
It seems all but lost.

Wild Sea

Take me away with you,
The rolling wind,
Through my bones,
You seem to know my soul.

Life has its ups and downs,
We have all had our share of heartache,
We soak it all up,
Try to forget,
The sea mends our broken hearts again and again.

We visit the sea,
To feel freedom from the sadness within,
It batters the coast,
The icy waters call me home,
It knows my heart,
That is where I belong.

Down by the sea,
The wailing sea,
Speaks to me,
Freely.

My mind soars,
I am young once more,
Me beside the sea,
As free as I can possibly be.

Suffering

You wear your suffering with pride,
You like to show it all around,
You suffer about things that never change,
Then when they do,
The crying remains.

So things have changed,
They will never be the same again,
You didn't choose it to be this way.

Your suffering expands,
Grows some more,
Until you don't know what to do at all,
You do what you know,
You suffer some more,
On and on it goes,
This is the life you chose!

Older

Oh how we begged to be older,
We prayed for the day we were eighteen,
Then it was twenty-one,
Now look at us!

All tired and forlorn,
Why did we pray for this?
When we had it all.

From the day we are born,
We are dying inside,
This is the life we have been thrown,
We try our best,
Onwards we must go.

Who Are You?

Who are you?
Beneath the hair,
Beneath this skin?
Who are you really?
What lurks within?

Your eyes tell your life story,
You try to hide behind a frown,
Sometimes a laugh,
I see it all, though,
I see your heart has been shattered a thousand times.

You try to keep the faith,
Each day seems harder,
More chaos than ever before,
What happened earlier on?
Only God really knows.

You are more than the tales you tell,
The funny stories you like to regale,
Oh people think you have it all,
Inside you feel you have nothing at all.

No self-confidence at all,
You hide behind your face,
You use it as a mask,
To hide all the pain,
Maybe that's why you love to walk in the rain,
You feel as though you can escape everything.

The Moon

If you are lonely,
Think of the moon,
Look to the stars,
Someone out there is staring up at it too,
Thinking of you,
Of all that you do.

Power

All you doubters,
I persevered,
I worked hard,
I made myself into what I am today.

Your snide comments mean nothing to me,
I never listened to you back then,
Why would I listen now?

I had the power,
I needed nobody else,
Just myself minus the innocence.

Solo

You obsess over the past,
You digress over the future,
If only you knew the power you store,
Within yourself,
You would never feel the need,
To search for more.

You have everything you need,
Stored within your soul,
You need nobody,
Only yourself in the solo role,
You are the Captain of this ship,
So sail it some more.

That Smile

That smile hides a multitude of sins,
Nobody sees what hides underneath,
They don't understand the pain you feel,
That laugh hides everything.

You continue to be jovial,
You hide yourself some more,
You keep it all to yourself,
You like to hide your broken soul.

What Have You Got?

Acting all high and mighty,
Where does that get you?
Alone and cold,
That's where you find yourself,
Out on your own,
You don't care, though.

Busy talking about cash-flow,
Nobody prays for health anymore,
They beg for some money and maybe a nice car,
How vacuous we all are.

People coming for you,
Drag you from your ivory tower,
You bolted yourself in long ago.

They will never smell your fear,
Lone wolf,
No friends here,
Not really,
Tough as old nails,
They won't see how you bleed.

What have you really got?
When it all boils down to it?
A lot of debt I would guess,
Hangers-on,
They won't leave you,
Until the money runs out,
Then what you got?

Until then everyone wants a piece of you,
You know the truth, though,
They don't really like you,
They just want a leg up,
So, now what have you really got?

It's hard being you,
Nobody actually likes you,
They just want to own you,
You won't let that happen, though,
So, now what have you really got?
Not much.

Isolated and alone,
It's sad being you,
Locked in your ivory home,
You're too tired to care,
Too desolate to feel the despair.

Wedding

A wedding is but one day,
The commitment of a lifetime,
Promises of forever,
You and I,
Beside the sea,
Loving life.

Wedding rings symbolise eternal love,
Never take them off,
That's the advice my mother gave,
Remember you are only half of a whole now,
Wear that ring until you are old.

'Til death do us part,
Spend your days having fun,
Loving one another never gets dull.

Vacuous

Words,
Only words,
Baseless,
Vacant words.

You say them,
They mean nothing at all,
They exit your mouth at the speed of light,
Nothingness pursues you,
It must be difficult being as vacuous as you.

Quietly

Let them go,
Quietly,
They didn't mean anything at all,
Happy to steal pieces of you until dawn,
You don't need that at all,
With that, they were gone.

Swan

I think of you,
My heart still feels sad,
To know you never really knew what you had.

You cast me aside,
Wrecked my colours,
Crumpled me up,
You thought nobody could love me.

You were wrong,
My beauty shines on,
Maybe you cannot see it,
Not now.

A new love came along,
Seen me for what I was,
Not an ugly duckling but a swan,
My colours sparkle on.

Time

Time is running out for us,
You waste your time on idle things,
Can't you hear the ticking of the clock?
You have no idea how long you've got,
Stop wasting your time on things that matter not
one jot.

Stubborn

Your stubborn heart,
Refuses to give up,
It shall not quit,
You keep going,
Sometimes you want to throw it all in,
The fear of having no aspirations at all,
Propels you on.

Perfection

You have stabbed me in the back multiple times,
Thinking I do not know,
How silly are you?
I choose to ignore the bad things you like to do,
I know karma is a harsh master,
You shall taste what you sow.

I choose to do good,
Whilst you prefer to backstab and act lewd,
Go ahead,
Time and fate shall soon spoon feed you,
All the meanness you have accrued.

The urge to be perfect,
Deserts me every morn,
The realisation that perfection is lost on me,
It's a pointless task,
So now that urge has gone.

Mask

I have reached the end of my rope,
The end of my tether,
I can be no more,
Nor any less than I am.

If you do not like me,
For all that I am,
Then it's your loss,
Not mine.

I've tried my best over the years,
To be this,
To be that,
Nothing ever lasted,
Only kindness remained.

I can only be what I am,
I am tired of the masks I have used,
So nowadays I have decided,
I shall just be myself,
I don't care to be anything else.

Oceans

Oceans apart,
Quietness invades the days,
Lack of communication,
The love has faded away.

Years ago,
That wasn't the way,
You know that better than most,
What happened to us?

Nothing left,
Just dead air,
White noise,
That's what makes it all the more of a surprise.

We are dead in the water now,
Darkness all around,
To see what has happened to us,
You seem nonplussed,
That's what makes it all the more absurd.

Pictures

All you left me with,
The photographs I like to stare at,
The memories,
They chase me still,
Unabated,
They still make me catch my breath.

Thinking back to days gone by,
Those days have passed,
Never to return again,
So now I have the pictures,
They help me remember you.

That's all I have of you,
Nothing else remains,
Just the pictures in my brain,
That I play nonstop of you.

Nobody can take my memories,
They are mine to keep,
As vivid as can be,
Flash up at random times,
Makes me feel the pain once again,
It always stays the same.

Thankful

Thank you for these days,
For another blessed day,
For the fresh air,
The wind in my hair.

I no longer care if I look a mess,
If you do not like the clothes I wear,
Whether you dislike the lilt in my voice,
You hate my accent.

I care no more,
It is no accident,
I do what I like,
When I like,
Nobody controls me,
I do as I please,
Refrain from judging me, please.

I know what matters,
What lays in my heart,
I do not care if you think me too plump,
I am nice.

I am delighted for the little arms that surround me,
The tiny kisses that wake me up,
The cuddles that I feel,
The love that I give.

I am happy with the sun in the sky,
The rain on my face,

The water in my bath,
The coffee in my cup,
The love in my heart.

Thank you, God,
For I have lived,
If I die tomorrow I know that I give with an open heart,
My love is eternal,
That shall never depart,
We shall never truly be apart.

Pointless

There is no point arguing with you,
You believe all that you say,
All that you do,
You believe to be true.

You do not realise there is no truth in your words,
You tell lies,
As if they are going out of fashion,
One leads to another.

You believe your words to be the truth,
It makes me sad for you,
You know not what you do.

Oops

Oh me,
Oh my,
What just popped out of my mouth?

I'm sorry I can't lie,
Honesty comes easily to me,
You don't like the words I drop,
Not my fault.

Don't blame me,
I just say,
Whatever enters my mind,
My mouth shouts them out,
Not said in spite,
Of that you may never be in doubt.

The Journey

Don't keep waiting for the happy ending,
It may never come,
How about you focus on the story along the way?

Instead of fixating on the happy ending,
Concentrate on making every piece of your life,
As fun as can be,
As exciting as it can be.

Don't waste your time,
Nor your life,
Waiting for something that may never arrive.

Make the journey special,
Then happiness will come,
No matter what the outcome.

Leave You

I wave you goodbye,
With a sad smile,
You cannot keep up,
Too busy by far,
So I shall leave you behind,
Until you feel the need to catch up.

I won't forget you,
You will always be imprinted on my mind,
Until we meet again,
That's when we shall see each other, my friend.

Reject

Doors slam,
You are unhappy,
I have let you down.

You are ashamed,
I can only berate myself,
I feel so helpless.

I am exhausted with it all,
I don't mean to let it all go,
I am flawed.

The madness,
The unpleasantness,
It stinks,
I cry some more,
This is not what I came for.

I fall to the floor,
I want to whine and groan,
I realise I am alone.

I never said I was perfect,
If only you knew,
I wish I were brand new,
Maybe I could start again,
Learn differently?

When did I become like this?
I have become the person I detest,
There are no benefits.

Makes me lose the will to live,
Civil unrest,
Is alive and well,
Oh how I reject myself.

A DREAMER OF IMPROBABLE DREAMS...

Sweet Dreams

Sweet dreams my friends,
We shall meet again.

In the land of nod,
Sleep takes our hand,
Walks us down a winding path.

Magic appears,
When sleep is near,
Never fear.

Eyes

Look deep into the eyes,
The gateway to the soul,
What can you see lurking there?

I see spirits galore,
Watching over you,
Making sure you soar.

One Last Time

If only I could go back,
Ring you back,
Hear your voice one last time.

I cannot change anything at all,
Though I wish I could,
I would do it all,
Just to hear your voice,
Singing in my ears,
One last time,
Tell you how loved you are.

I love you so,
In your heart,
I know you know.

Learn

I do not need anyone else,
I have learned to depend on myself,
Be my own best friend.

I'm tired of being everyone's second best,
I should be a first choice,
I'm just as good as everyone else.

At least this way I know I understand myself,
I won't hurt myself,
I can prioritise myself,
Make me number one,
At long last, I can finally come first.

It's as though everyone else has forgotten about me,
That's okay because I have me, myself and I,
I can depend on me.

I don't need any other soul,
I wish I had learned this sooner,
Instead of waiting until I am almost forty,
So much time wasted on crying and whining,
I should have just changed my mind-set,
Made myself come first for once,
To hell with everybody else.

Tell Me

Kiss me,
Hold me tight,
One more time,
Tell me I'm your light,
Once more,
Make everything alright.

Tied

Our hearts have a connection,
Nobody else comes close,
We have known each other in every life,
Our heart strings are tied,
For every day of our lives.

The Heart

I would know you anywhere,
In a hurricane,
In murky waters,
Even within the eye of a tornado,
I would know you still.

I have known you in a million lives,
Thousands of times,
I have known your love,
I would know you anywhere,
Even now,
I know your soul.

The heart understands more than most,
It feels you,
Long before the eyes see you.

The heart can hear you,
Knows your sounds,
Understands your touch,
Our souls have been entwined for so long,
We just know.

You Two

I walk beside you every day,
Loving you every second,
In every moment that prevails.

You are my daughter,
My life,
The world revolves around you,
Your baby brother too.

Remember when I am gone,
I will walk beside you still,
Just as my mother does for me now,
Stop that crying,
Be strong,
Do that for me.

Be courageous,
Be kind,
Show compassion in your heart,
Let it shine out of your eyes,
Most of all,
Make yourself proud.

God bless you two,
My babies,
Both the apples of my eyes.

I will love you both,
This will continue,
Long after I have died.

Pregnant

I feel you within,
Growing stronger every day,
I know you hear my words,
You like my singing,
Maybe it's the tone of my voice?

You will be here soon enough,
Then I will be able to hold you,
You will feel my touch.

We love you already,
We are as delighted as can be,
Oh how blessed are we?
To be expecting another little baby,
To join our already amazing little family.

God bless you little baby,
May God protect you and bring you to me,
Until then rest easily,
Knowing Mummy shall protect you.

Whilst you lay in slumber,
We all love you already,
When you come out,
We shall all be ready,
Kisses and cuddles await you,
Don't be frightened,
We all adore you.

Staring

She is more than these scars,
Her flaws weighed her down,
Made her who she was,
Whilst everyone else is looking down,
She is busy staring at the stars.

Love Your Life

Love the life you live,
Start today,
Then you may win,
Give it your all,
Forget the sins,
Love the life you lead,
Watch your life begin.

No More

I won't chase you anymore,
Those days have gone,
I've slammed that door.

If you want me,
You know where I am,
Always accessible,
Though I know you don't care to try.

So we leave it,
The years continue to fly by,
Until one day,
One of us will eventually die,
By then it's too late to cry.

Warrior Queen

Broken and bruised,
A fantasy misused,
She was a warrior queen,
She had won every battle at every place she had ever been.

Glint

They look at you,
A glint in their eye,
Watch you as you pass by,
There's something magical about you,
You cannot see,
Everybody is busy watching you being you,
Quietly judging.

Over

Years have passed us by,
The way time has left us,
Is not a pretty sight.

We kept our laughter,
We threw away the tears,
I know you still think of me,
Even after all these years.

We cannot rewind time,
Nor erase the mistakes we made,
We leave them in the past,
As we use up all our days.

Love lived here once,
The fire burned bright,
Then one day you just got up,
You'd had enough,
You just walked out.

It took years to bandage my heart,
The holes caused me anguish,
Even now the splinters hurt me,
Cause me pain.

As I sit in my rocking chair,
I close my eyes,
I see your face crystal clear,
As if you are still here.

I know I wasn't perfect,
We both caused the arguments,
The havoc that ensued,
I still cannot get over,
Never seeing you.

No fond farewells,
No long goodbyes,
You exited my life,
As if you were a butterfly.

Up and Down

I have no idea why I am this way,
One day up,
One day down,
No two are the same.

Cannot seem to get my head out of the clouds,
Then other days I perish within the rain,
I feel every heavy drop,
It soaks me thoroughly until I am numb.

I wish I could escape the hurricanes,
The ones that reside in my brain,
Sadly they remain.

I wish I could find the sunshine in the darkest of days,
Though sometimes it refuses to play.

Tomorrow is another day,
So until then I will cling to today,
Then I shall start again,
Hopefully not the same way,
Today I feel like sailing away.

Love You

Nobody can tear us apart,
Try as they may,
We know the truth,
The way it was,
Right from the very start,
We know the facts,
Nothing shall rip us apart.

No gossip,
No lies,
No big stories,
The ones they like to tell all the time.

We smile,
We nod,
We know the truth, though,
It pours from our hearts.

Forever friends,
Nobody can take that away,
Try as they may,
Our friendship remains the same way.

I still love you,
Nobody can take that away,
That's how I feel,
I know you feel the same way.

Stop

When we stop trying,
Stop looking for the rainbows,
Oh the things we finally see,
Oh how happy we shall be,
Just you and me.

Twin Flames

We were once part of the same coal,
The same fire,
We burned some more,
We roared.

Then we were embers by the moonlight sky,
We floated up high,
Became part of the sky,
We reached the stars,
We sparkled some more.

We meet time and time again,
We are twin flames,
We find one another again and again.

Our love is bright,
We know we are a match,
Always, at first sight,
Our hearts know they are attached.